Geta Toss

Bonnie Ferrante

ISBN 978-1-928064-39-8
Copyright June 28, 2017
© Bonnie Ferrante

Character Concept Illustrator
Rebecca Pucci

Published February 27, 2018

Even though they looked nothing alike, everyone called Emily and Maria "The Twins." They weren't sisters but they played together, shared their lunches, and slept over at each other's house. They were the only girls their age on the street.

a new family moved in. The girl did not look like Maria. She did not look like Emily.

At school, the teacher introduced the new girl, Yuko from Japan. Yuko knew English but she did not sound the same as the other girls.

Yuko said, "Here, children come in many sizes, shapes and colours."

Emily looked around the room. She saw Maria smile at Yuko. Emily frowned.

In writing class, the students shared.
Emily shared about biking.
Maria shared about dancing.
Yuko shared about missing her best friend,
Chieyko who parted her hair in the middle
like Yuko's, was the same size, and wore
a black ojuzu on her left wrist.

"What's an ojuzu?" asked Maria.

Yuko held up her left arm showing a grey beaded bracelet with two smaller beads and one larger one. It was tied with a loop.

"That's pretty," said Maria.

At recess, Emily and Maria watched Yuko play ball. When Yuko smiled at them, Emily took Maria's hand and pulled her to the monkey bars.

Yuko played alone.

The next day, Emily and Maria played Rock, Paper, Scissors.

"I know that game," Yuko said. "*Jan Ken Poi*. She made scissors with her thumb and finger.

"It's like this," said Emily as she pointed her first two fingers.

"When it is a tie, said Yuko, "then we do *Achi Mitte Hoi*. I can show you."

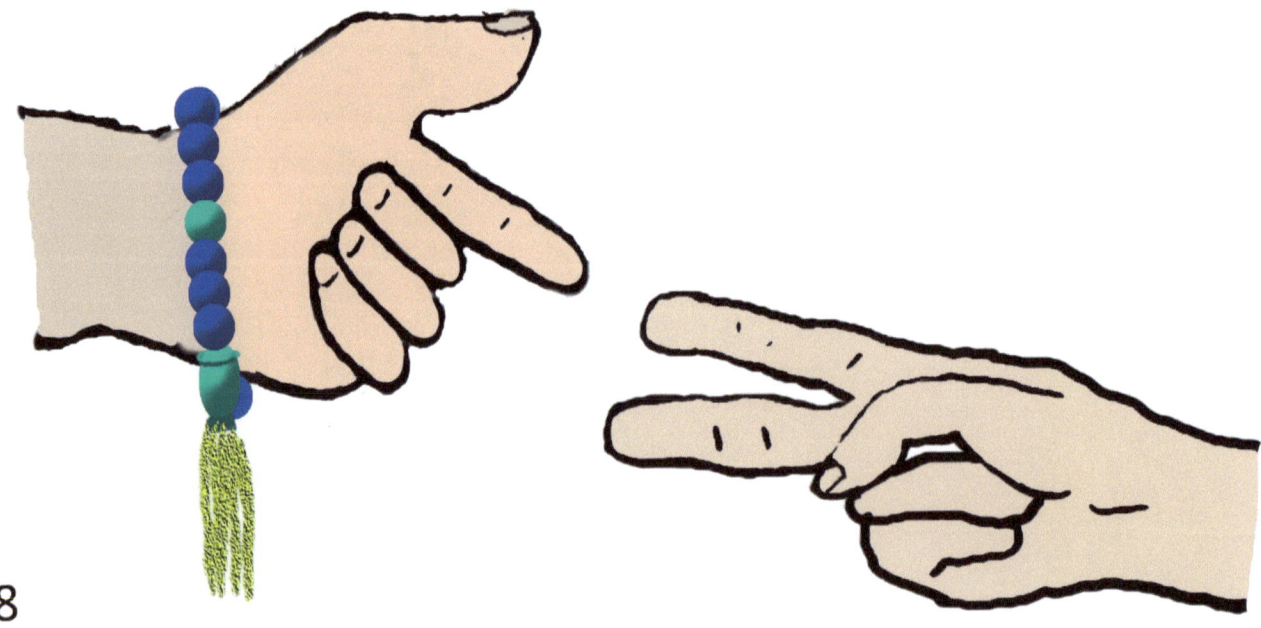

"No, thanks," said Emily. She took Maria's hand and they ran to join a soccer game.

Yuko played alone.

The next day during lunch Emily ate a pea butter sandwich while Maria stood in line to warm up her pasta.

Yuko heated rice with soya sauce, tofu, red chopped ginger and sesame seeds.

"That smells funny," said Emily.

"My Obachan made it," explained Yuko. "My grandmother."

Maria nodded. "I make gnocci with my grandmother."

Emily tugged Maria's shirt and led her to her desk.

Yuko ate alone.

After school, Maria and Emily walked home together. Ahead of them, Yuko dragged her feet.

"Her brother must be away today," Maria said.

They watched Yuko stop, bend over, and loosen the Velcro on her shoe. She shouted in Japanese and kicked her shoe into the air.

Maria's eyes widened.
"Did you see that?" she asked.

Yuko hopped to her shoe, stuck her foot into it, and kicked it into the air, yelling another word.

"What are you doing?" asked Maria.

"I'm playing geta toss," said Yuko as she picked up her shoe.

"I know caber toss," said Emily, "But, what's geta toss?"

"I guess how the shoe will land. Right side up or upside down. My Obachan used to play it with her geta, wooden sandles, from long ago."

"Neat," said Maria.
She untied her right shoe.

Emily frowned.

"If one girl plays," said Yuko, "she shouts 'top up' or 'bottom up'. If two play, we say 'odd' or 'even'."

"Even," said Maria.

"Toss!" said Yuko.

The shoes landed bottom up.

"We win!" shouted Maria.

They hopped to their shoes. Maria put her hand into Yuko's and then reached for Emily. Emily wiped her tears.

"What's wrong?" asked Maria.

"Are you still going to be my friend?"

Maria held out her hand. "Forever."

Emily wiped her cheeks, loosened her shoe, and took Maria's hand.

Yuko said, "If three play, we say if most shoes will be 'top up' or 'bottom up'."

"Tops up," Emily said.

"Toss!" shouted Yuko.

The girls shouted, kicked, hopped, and laughed. A delivery truck rounded the corner.

"Toss!" shouted Yuko.

The smallest shoe flew onto the road.

The truck's front wheel drove over the shoe. It made a tire mark on Yuko's runner and one side was split open.

"Your parents are going to be mad," said Emily.

Yuko put on her shoe and rubbed the mark.

"We'll help you tell them," said Maria.

Yuko's parents were outside. The two girls held Yuko's arms as they approached. Yuko's eyes were wet with tears.

"Has something happened?" asked her father.

Yuko lifted her foot. Mr. Takamoto dropped his rake. "A car has run over Yuko's foot!" he shouted.

Mrs. Takamoto dropped a towel and ran over. She spoke in quick Japanese.

"It's okay," said Emily. "She's not hurt."

Maria explained.

"At least her foot wasn't in it," said Mr. Takamoto.

"We can buy a new shoe but not a new foot," said Mrs. Takamoto.

Yuko's grandmother came out with a plate.
"Ocashi?" she said.

"Cookies," said Yuko.

"There are different kinds," said Maria. "Let's get a toss. Odd one out gets to pick first."

From that day on, the "The Triplets" loved geta toss. Maria and Emily's parents never understood why their girls had such badly scuffed shoes.

Yuko always had some one to play with.

Follow-up Questions

Maria is friendly to Yuko but Emily keeps pulling her away. How do you think Yuko felt being left out? What could Maria have done differently?

Shin Buddhists wear an ojuzu on their wrists. What other items do people wear to show they follow a certain religion?

Geta shoes are easier to kick off than shoes with laces which tend to land top up. You can play a game similar to geta toss with coins. When one person plays, what is the probability of getting top up? When two people play, what is the probability of getting the same resullt? When three people play, what is the probability of getting one different?

Variations of rock, paper, scissors are played all over the world. Can you create a similar game not using rock, paper, or scissors?

On page 19, Emily becomes upset. Why? What did she think was going to happen? How does this explain her behavior toward Yuko?

Do you have a special game from your culture that you can share with your friends? Can you learn and share a game from another culture?

www.ingramcontent.com/pod-product-compliance
Lightning Source LLC
Chambersburg PA
CBHW042127040426
42450CB00002B/95